Written by Penny Boxall

Illustrated by
Lia Visirin

hachette
LEARNING

Hachette UK's policy is to use papers that are natural, renewable and recyclable products and made from wood grown in well-managed forests and other controlled sources. The logging and manufacturing processes are expected to conform to the environmental regulations of the country of origin.

ISBN: 9781036000615

Text © Penny Boxall

Illustrations, design and layout © 2025 Hodder & Stoughton Limited
First published in 2025 by Hachette Learning,
An Hachette UK Company
Carmelite House, 50 Victoria Embankment, London EC4Y 0DZ

www.HachetteLearning.com

The authorised representative in the EEA is Hachette Ireland, 8 Castlecourt Centre, Dublin 15, D15 XTP3, Ireland (email: info@hbgi.ie)

Impression number 10 9 8 7 6 5 4 3 2 1

Year 2029 2028 2027 2026 2025

Author: Penny Boxall
Series Editor: Catherine Coe
Illustrator: Lia Visirin / Advocate Art
Educational Reviewer: Pauline Allen
Page layouts: Kamae Design

With thanks to the schools that took part in the development of Reading Planet *Cosmos*, including: Ancaster CE Primary School, Ancaster; Downsway Primary School, Reading; Ferry Lane Primary School, London; Foxborough Primary School, Slough; Griffin Park Primary School, Blackburn; St Barnabas CE First & Middle School, Pershore; Tranmoor Primary School, Doncaster; and Wilton CE Primary School, Wilton.

The Publishers would like to thank the following for permission to reproduce copyright material.
p35 © Nadzeya Pakhomava/stock.adobe.com

All rights reserved. Apart from any use permitted under UK copyright law, no part of this publication may be reproduced or transmitted in any form or by any means, electronic or mechanical, including photocopying and recording, or held within any information storage and retrieval system, without permission in writing from the publisher or under licence from the Copyright Licensing Agency Limited. Further details of such licences (for reprographic reproduction) may be obtained from the Copyright Licensing Agency Limited, www.cla.co.uk

A catalogue record for this title is available from the British Library.

Printed in the UK

To order please visit www.HachetteLearning.com or contact Customer Service at education@hachette.co.uk / +44 (0)1235 827827

Contents

Chapter 1 4

Chapter 2 9

Chapter 3 14

Chapter 4 21

Chapter 5 27

Chapter 6 36

Chapter 7 44

Chapter 8 52

Chapter 9 59

Chapter 1

Elsa can't remember anything about this place,
though Dad says she has been before.
The buildings flash by through the windows of the tram.
All the houses here are the colours of sweets,
or the icing on little cakes.
Even this winter sky looks different from the winter sky
above her home city.
In London, the clouds are polite and faraway and grey;
here, they're fat with snow.
It's chilly and strange, and *just not home*;
and it's the Christmas holidays!
Elsa's friend Aisha is not just round the corner here.
She says, 'How long do we have to stay?'

Dad doesn't answer at first,
and Elsa thinks he might be worried,
or a tiny bit cross, or maybe both,
like he was on the plane, and later on the bus.

But at last he replies, 'I don't know, petal.
Just as long as Grandma needs us.'
Elsa has to be content with that.

She watches a snowflake land on the tram's window-glass,
then melt, and make its wet way down the pane.
She feels like she could almost be that piece of snow:
neither one place nor the other.

They get off the tram, and Dad leads Elsa
down one narrow street after another, until …
'There it is,' he points.
The main square isn't far but it feels a hundred miles,
a hundred *years* away. Elsa squints to see the red door
in its side-street filled with shadows.

'Down there? In that *dark street*?' she says.
Dad looks at her and gives her a quick squeeze.

'Now, Elsa, you're getting too big to be afraid
of the dark, aren't you, love?'

Elsa squirms from under his arm.
'I'm not *afraid*! It's just …' She doesn't finish,
thinking of how the night-time seems to gather
all the skittery, creepy things that vanish in the day.
She shrugs, and follows Dad down to the door.
'This is where *you* grew up?'

'Yep,' says Dad proudly. 'This is where I was a boy!'

Elsa looks at the door uncertainly,
and at the shop-sign with its carved and painted puppet,
dangling above the shadowed doorway. 'You grew up in a *toyshop*?'

Dad's searching in his coat pockets for something,
and seems a bit distracted. 'Sure. You don't remember coming here?
I suppose you weren't very old. Teeny-tiny, in fact!'

Elsa thinks she'd *definitely* have remembered a place like this,
but the memory is so slippery
it is like a wriggling fish, and she can't keep hold of it.
She has a little flash of something – Grandma's smile?
Or a magic trick that made her laugh?
'Your grandma just loved showing you the toyshop –
all the things she sold.'
Dad has found the key,
and now he's fumbling with the lock.

Elsa peers through the unlit window at the teddies, yoyos,
wooden bears and painted dolls in the display.
It all looks ... so *ancient*. 'People *bought* this stuff?'

'Don't be rude,' says Dad, and gives her a wink.
'Kids didn't have all fancy toys and games
when I was growing up, you know.'
By now he's wrestled the door open, and Elsa can see
a glimpse of stairs going straight up from the hallway.
'They lead to the flat,' Dad says. 'That's where we'll stay ...'
To the left is another door. 'It goes to the shop.' Dad smiles.
'Have a little look around, Explorer Elsa. On you go.'

It's like a sort of ancient jumble-sale.
Elsa brushes a finger along a shelf;
at once, the finger is all grey with dust,
as if it's turned to stone. But it's beautiful in here.

Dangling from the ceiling's beams are puppets –
marionettes in blasts of colour,
red-white-yellow-pink-green-orange-black-purple-blue.
And gold and silver – lots of it!
The ceiling is painted with stars.
Elsa shakes a shiver-tingle down her spine.

'Elsa?' calls Dad, from upstairs.
She hurries up the gloom-filled steps,
following the bright light of his voice.

'Dad?' She finds him in a bedroom
at the top of the flat, with a little neat bed,
a skylight in the beams,
and a comfortable chair. Elsa sniffs –
it smells unfamiliar, but quite nice, like dried flowers.

'There you are, my love.
Give me a hand with this, would you?' says Dad,
unfurling a string of fairy lights he must have brought from home.
'We'll hang them up on the beams,
so it'll look like your room.
And you can use Grandma's slippers. They're under the bed.'

Elsa grins. 'Thanks, Dad.' She holds the plug while Dad climbs
on a chair, and when they switch the lights on
the room looks cosier, more mysterious – even a bit magic.

Chapter 2

It's quiet in the flat.
They've not long arrived, and Dad is already getting ready
for the hospital and Grandma.
He tells Elsa that Grandma's neighbour Dagmara is just next door.
Elsa remembers her from when she visited them in London:
Dagmara has a lot of curly hair and a nice smile.
'If there's anything you need, my love – anything at all –
just give her a shout,' says Dad,
and then he leaves.

Elsa tries playing with some toys in the toyshop,
but they don't quite fit her mood.
By the time Dad comes back for lunch,
she's fizzing with unspent energy.
Dad heats up soup in the microwave,
telling her: 'Your grandma
seemed okay, I think. But I'm glad we're here.
How was your morning, love?'

'Boring! Dad, can't we go exploring?
Outside, in the city, I mean.'

Dad looks at his watch, mouth full of soup.
'I need to get back to the hospital ...'

'*Already?*' Elsa splutters. 'You've only just come in!'

But it's useless. He's already putting on his coat again,
already halfway out the door again,
already somewhere else again,
seeming to see something she can't see.
'Sweetheart, I've really got to dash. There's milk in the fridge.
And cookies on the counter.
I'll be back this afternoon.
And any time you need some help
or just some company, go get Dagmara.'

'But, Dad – I want more time with *you*.
Can't I come and visit Grandma with you?'

'Sorry, petal – not just yet.'
And then he's gone
and there's nothing else until it's 3pm.

When Dad comes in this time, Elsa frowns.
'Sorry I'm later than I meant to be, sweetheart,' he says,
like he doesn't notice her bad mood.
'Here, I got us pancakes on the way back home –
sorry they're a little cold. We can heat them in the microwave.'

As Elsa eats, she asks, 'Dad, can I go outside tomorrow?'
She thinks of the city she's only glimpsed,
its shadowy cobbled streets.

Now Dad frowns. 'Elsa, you don't know the city here ...'

'But, Dad! I can use a map!'

'No, kid. Not when I'm not here,' says Dad,
his frown matching hers.
'And saying that – I've got to dash.'

'But, Dad! *When* will you be here?'

'I'm sorry. I can't help it,' says Dad.
'Please, think of Grandma, too.
Won't you help me out, and her, by being good?'
He leaves her with a kiss on the top of her head.

Being good is the thing that Elsa is so often asked to do.
So why is it that *being good* can feel so boring, and so bad?

She longs for Aisha's company,
writing her an only-in-her-head message.

> I wish we were home in London,
> peering through the Christmas windows.
> I wish we were
> scoffing chestnuts
> by the carousel.
> I wish we were
> skating, making jokes,
> being NORMAL.
> I wish – I wish – I wish …

She can *almost* imagine Aisha's answers,
but imagining is not the same as real.

So now, late in the afternoon, she flomps on the bed,
watching the last of the daylight flicker,
like a dying candle. *Great*, she thinks.
Now there's just darkness to look forward to …
It's so unfair! It's the *Christmas holidays*!

And at once it's fully dark outside,
and she's still on her narrow bed,
under the dusty, shadowy beams
which glitter with her fairy lights.
Lying on her back, watching through the grimy sky-light,
she can see more flakes of snow begin to fall.
Softly, softly now – just a few at first. Then more and more,
until in not much time at all the sky-light has filled with snow,
and Elsa's staring at nothing but blank glass …
And she drifts, like snowflakes, into sleep.

She can't say when she can first hear voices downstairs.
They filter in like mist through the forests of her dreams.
Dad must be back. But who's that he's talking to?
Elsa rubs her eyes, flicks on her bedside lamp,
lights up a little island in the fairy-lit sea of her room.
She slips on Grandma's slippers over her thick socks.

Grandma.
It's barely more than a word to her –
she knows Grandma so little.
Elsa was only tiny when they last made the trip to this city.
But she's seen the care and worry in Dad's eyes,
and she knows that Grandma is his own mum,
and she hugs *that* word tight.

Grandma's slippers fit. That seems funny, somehow –
that a ten-year-old and an *eighty*-year-old
should have the same size feet.
She feels like feet should keep growing and growing …
Elsa makes her way carefully downstairs.

Funny that Dad hasn't put the hall-light on.
He usually does that at home.
Elsa listens for the voices again, but for now they've stopped.

She pauses in the hall. There's a little bit of light
like spilled milk seeping under the door from the shop.
Curious, Elsa pushes the door, and creeps in.

Chapter 3

She sees a sort of flickering, a shifting of the shadows.
And cutting through that strange dream-candlelight
is someone's voice. It is whisper-sharp,
paper-thin, as bright as the moon.

It says: *Elsa? Elsa?*

Elsa is not afraid of the voice.
She knows it like she knows the voice of her own heart,
but she could not tell you why.

It's coming from a corner of the shop,
where the light is flickering strongest.
There's something like a big TV there,
a box of glowing light; but this is no TV.

Little shapes of darkness are twirling in the light.
And words come to her mind, from somewhere:
shadow theatre. Someone must have left it plugged in,
turned on at the wall, or something. Strange!

But she settles down in front of it,
cross-legged on the carpet,
and watches the shadows dance and play:
little shadow shapes that seem to be part of a story ...
There, a little shadow boy and a bigger shadow girl
are walking near a wintry forest,
and the girl carries a basket of bread,
which she swings in her hand.

And Elsa realises, as she watches them,
that they're from a story she knows well …

Shadow Hansel takes Shadow Gretel by the hand,
and together they wander off towards the Shadow Forest.

(Elsa can *sort of* tell the forest is nothing more than
strips of thin paper for branches and thorns. But somehow,
gazing into that shimmering light, it *could*, almost, be real.)

Shadow Gretel breaks apart her shadow bread,
throwing shadow crumbs behind her, on the path.
But shadow birds swoop down from the shadowed sky,
like paper aeroplanes, and gobble up the trail
behind the children's backs.

Yes, Elsa knows what's happening:
they're getting lost inside the wood.
They'll find the witch's cottage soon ... And sure enough:

The sun is setting. Sunset-colours flood the sky;
the gloom begins to seep inside the shadow forest.
What will the children do? There – Gretel points:
a cosy cottage at the heart of the forest. She hurries towards it.

Elsa leans forward, looking closely at the cottage.

The door creaks ajar, and the light spills out. It is a glittering light,
like frost. Gretel steps inside the cottage; Hansel waits outside.
And waits.   And waits.   And waits.   And waits.   And waits.

But this bit is different, surely?
Elsa thinks that it was supposed to be Hansel, not the girl,
who goes inside the cottage first?
And the wicked witch should capture *him*,
and then his brave sister will help get him out?

Elsa wonders what could happen now.

But something is changing in the shadow wood:
it's darkening still further.
The light that spilled from the cottage-door is acting oddly,
not like light at all – instead, like *cold*.
It's freezing on the paper ground.
The shadow trees have grown thick frost on them ...
Hansel stands unmoving on the spot.
And as the paper moon rises round and shining
in the deep-blue paper sky, something flits in front of it!
The shape is something shadowed, jagged,
something sharp and dangerous as ice ...

Elsa has a feeling like moths in her stomach, excited-jittery.
That jagged thing has gone, but still the Shadow Hansel waits.
The cottage door is standing open, and the frost
is spreading over everything ... And now something else appears:
lines of letters, floating across the moonlit, clouded sky.
Elsa leans forward to read them:

All through the magic Shadowlands
a frosty villain creeps.
An endless winter settles here
and sends us all to sleep.

And then the shadow theatre set goes dark,
as if a candle-flame's been snuffed right out.

Elsa's sitting in the dark, cross-legged on the carpet.
She stands up, races to the doorway, feels for the light switch,
and floods the room with light.

Phew!

But that's odd – if the lights are still working,
whatever stopped the shadow play wasn't a power-cut,
and it ended the story just when she was fascinated
by the glittery shadow world.

And at that moment the front door is thrown open
and Elsa scrunches up, a little spooked.
Then, on the other side of the door, it's

Dad.

She feels a **w h o o s h** of relief.

'Elsa, darling. Everything OK? I saw the light come on …
Why were you sitting here in the dark?!'

Elsa finds she can't exactly explain. The shadow play was *hers*.
'Uhmmmm … I was … reading.'

'Reading in the dark?! How exactly does *that* work?
Well, anyway, I brought us pierogis.
Let's eat them while they're hot.'

Elsa follows him upstairs to the flat.
'Pierogis? What's that?'

Dad smiles. 'Try one. You'll see.'

'Thanks, Dad.'
She bites one of the little parcels of dough, uncertainly,
and steam and lovely hot cheese bubble out. 'Yum!'
Dad is comforting; pierogis are comforting.
She gives Dad a small hug, her mouth full of delicious pierogi,
and looks up at his tired face. She asks,
'How's Grandma today?'

Dad waits a second, like he doesn't know the words.
'Grandma ... Well, Grandma isn't very well, love. But she's tough.
Just ... just keep hoping for her, won't you?'
And his mouth closes like a door after the words he's just said.

Elsa half-remembers that long-ago smile of Grandma's.
So she gathers up every little bit of hope she can find,
like she's picking up bright shells of hope on the beach. She thinks:
I hope
I hope
I hope
even though she isn't exactly sure what it is that she is hoping for.

She turns back to her pierogis, and she thinks a message to Aisha:

> Everything's sort of
> upside-down here.
> I can't explain very well.
> I'll tell you more
> as soon as I get home.

And all the time she and Dad are eating,
her mind's flicking back to that shadow theatre,
the beautiful little silhouette house, the enticing shadow wood,
the strange way the story stopped,
and the mysterious shadowy feeling it gave her …

>And most of all,
>to that spiky shape
>flitting across the bright,
>wide eye of the moon.

Chapter 4

It's there next morning, too, the shadowy feeling –
as she brushes her teeth and looks in the mirror,
and then has breakfast:
a mug of warm milk with cinnamon, a piece of buttery toast.
Then Dad looks at his watch and she prickles,
thinking he has to go again, but instead he surprises her.
'Come on, pet – I'll show you round the town a bit.
I don't need to go to the hospital right away.
Let's clear the cobwebs, eh?'

Elsa doesn't need to be told twice.
She grabs her coat with the fluffy hood
and her thick gloves, a soft scarf, and her snow-boots,
and she's waiting by the door.
Dad laughs, seeing her ready so quick.
Then they step out to the frosted park.
It's a collection of snowy lawns with trees,
looping around the outskirts of the town
like a string of enormous, bright-white pearls.
There are geese in the park, too,
honking and complaining at the cold as they shiver,
lifting their orange feet.

Elsa has the perfect idea!

She scoops up a handful of snow and, before he realises,
pings it at Dad. He blinks, then laughs,
then pelts a snowball right back at her.

They battle for ten minutes, until Dad scoops Elsa up
as if she weighed the same as a snowball, and laughs,
'Alright! You win! You win! Come on, let's see the town.'

And he leads her through the park to the cobbled streets,
and the ancient wonky buildings in the old town,
and the main square. Elsa is in love with this place.
It's like being in a fairytale.
She almost expects to see the Three Bears
living in one of the wooden houses.
It all looks so ... unreal. But she can feel the sharp cold air,
the hint of more snow on the way.
And she smells the warm cooking-scent
of street food, wafting on the breeze.

'Do you remember all this, Dad? From when you were a kid?'

'Of course! How could I forget it? This place is the *best*.'

Elsa's puzzled. 'Then why did you leave it?
Why did you go to London?' But Dad's face
does that closed-door thing again, and he says,
'Sometimes we have to leave, even though we love somewhere.'
And Elsa doesn't really understand, but Dad's whole face
has shut tight now. He says it's time for them to get back,
time for him to go and check on Grandma.

And then before she knows it she's back in the small flat
over Grandma's toyshop, and the walls seem to lean in a bit
as Elsa waves Dad off again, with a little sigh.

When he's gone she trundles down the steps to the shop,
and looks round at the jumbled odds and ends.
It's still like a dream of a shop from the past.
She holds her breath and tiptoes. And when she's in the corner
at the back, the little theatre looks ... quite ordinary.
It's just a sheet of pale cloth with a cardboard frame around it
to make it look like a theatre.

There are no characters among the shadowy scenery.
It shows a blue-washed icy landscape, with a tangled forest
and a distant hill. In the folds of the hill stands a tower
made of pure shadow, which Elsa hasn't noticed before.

The trees have closed around the cottage and Hansel's nowhere to be seen. Feeling very silly, Elsa calls out once or twice, in a whisper, 'Hello ... Hello?' But she hears only her own voice in the empty room.

Elsa suddenly feels the need to DO SOMETHING. Something new.
She sees a stack of paper and some pencils on the shelf.
Beside them is an old pair of beautiful silver scissors.
Elsa grabs the lot.
She plonks down on the floor,
deciding to pass the time with some drawing.

'You've been busy!' says a voice.

Elsa looks round. She didn't hear Dagmara come in, she was so focused on her project.

Elsa turns back to her crafting. 'Oh, hi.'

'What are you making?' Dagmara asks, offering a chocolate from a bag.

Elsa finishes a careful bit of cutting-out, then takes a chocolate. 'Thanks. They're geese, like the ones I saw in the park with Dad.'

Dagmara picks up one of the paper shapes, smiling a big smile. 'They're great!'

Elsa smiles back. Then the front door opens, and Dad comes in, shaking snow from his hair. 'Hello, you two. Made friends?'

'Yep,' says Elsa, through a chocolate mouthful.

'These geese are good,' Dad says, picking one up.
'You've got talent, my child!'

'I know,' says Elsa. Dad snorts and ruffles her hair.

Then Dagmara says, 'Do you want to make your geese fly?'

Elsa doesn't know what Dagmara means,
but she's already dashed out to her flat.
She comes back with a ball of string
and a handful of pins with flat, double-points.
'Split-pins,' says Dagmara. 'For the wings.'
'How?' says Elsa. Dagmara shows her.

Picking up one goose, she cuts across its wings,
and pushes the pins through its body.
'Then you bend the two points over on the other side,' she says.
With a bit of string pushed through the paper wings
she can make it flap and scuffle. Elsa laughs, then copies,
quick as snow, on the next goose. 'They look so real! Thanks!'

Dagmara smiles and gets up to leave.
'Your grandma taught me how to do that!'

After dinner, Elsa and Dad stay up later than normal,
making more geese, until the carpet of the shop
is covered in beautiful little fragments: tiny flying paper geese
and scraps of off-cut paper, and bits of string, and happiness.

And somehow then it's time for bed.
Elsa drags her tired legs up the stairs to her room, switches off
the cosy bedside lamp, and snuggles down into her quilt
beneath the fairy lights. The wings of her paper geese
flap in her mind's eye as she drifts away to sleep.

Chapter 5

Voices again.

Elsa could *almost* still be dreaming
as she swings her legs over the side
of the bed, feels in the dark for her slippers, slips them on.
She could *almost* be sleepwalking. Past Dad's bedroom door ...
down the stairs ... What is it? Did she imagine it?
But sure enough there's the glow under the shop door,
and Elsa follows it to the back of the shop,
towards that strange TV-that-isn't-a-TV glow.
Towards the shadow theatre –

And
        then ...
                and
                      then ...
                              and
                                    then ...

The snow-bright paper moon sails high
upon a silver-speckled sky,
and shines its frozen lullaby.

The earth is frost, and wintry trees
criss-cross the paths like filigree.
The paper crows fly where they please.

Elsa's ... *in* the Shadowlands?
On paper legs and feet she stands,
and wonders at her paper hands ...

She scoops a ball of paper snow
(which feels both real and strange) and throws
it far – and hard as hard can be!
It shakes the branches of a tree.

A paper squirrel seems to wish
to play with her, and with a swish
of paper tail, it jumps and wriggles.
Elsa leaps and twirls and giggles.

It's fun, this land of paper games!
She scoops another snowball, aims
this one up high – into the air.
It breaks up into snowflakes there.

But then, like that, the squirrel's gone
and Elsa finds herself alone.
The land feels empty to her then.
She wishes for another friend.

She speaks, but words don't make a sound.
Instead, a paper scroll's unwound
above her head. There, in a cloud,
is what she meant to say out loud …

'Hansel? Hi …?' and 'Where am I?'
The letters punch into the sky.
No answer comes, except the sound
of footsteps on the paper ground –

but turning, she finds no one's there.
In fact, there's rustling everywhere …

Above the silvers, whites and blues,
the paper crows fly where they choose.

She looks down at the forking roads
to wood or hills, through paper snow.
One path is blank. The other's crossed
with footprints shining in the frost.

She thinks, 'Just standing here's no good!'
So choose she must. It's hills or wood.
She turns her back to mountainside –
it's blank and icy-cold. Besides,

she last saw Hansel *here*, and so
are those *his* footprints in the snow?
And that's the path – there's only one way in.
She shivers, rustling ... and

      follows

           him.

As soon as Elsa's in the snowy trees
it isn't really dark. Instead, she sees
a very strange and otherworldly sight:
a lantern glowing with a frost-blue light.

And as she walks, the branches hide the sky.
And as she walks, she listens, wondering why
the birds are quiet in these woods. And still
the lantern glows ahead: a light through chill.

She hurries in his footprints through the snow.
She'd thought it was as cold as it could go,
but all the while it's growing colder – how?
Quick! Hansel, with the lamp, is not far now ...

He's there, now, just ahead of her. 'Hey, Hans—'
Shivering, she reaches out a hand.
The stranger turns and stares. She judders back.
'Hansel? No ...' A frost-toothed grin ...

The stranger's hair's an avalanche,
his eyes are bright as snow.
His fingertips
are icy sticks;
his lantern coldly glows.

'Wandering, lonely, in my woods?
That isn't very wise!
I must insist
that you desist
before you – CRYSTALLISE!'

Elsa's frozen to the spot
by Jack's cold-glittery glare.
She wants to flee
but can't get free
from his bone-freezing stare.

He holds the lamp in his right hand,
an ... *ice cream* in his left!
He licks the drips
around his lips,
and sighs: *'Ice cream's THE BEST!'*

Before she knows what's happening
they're skating off at speed.
A glittering road
of ice and snow
is snaking through the trees ...

They've left the woods, and slipped away
towards the snowy slopes.
On top of it
a tower sits:
a place that freezes hope ...

Elsa wants to run, but can't ...
but when she gives a yell,
the sky is swarmed
with flying forms ...
They're ... something? ... she can't tell ...

Not paper bats or paper swans ...
But not just anything ...
She laughs ... *they're geese!*
Her paper geese!
They're flapping paper wings!

And on the back of one of them
is *Hansel*, swooping high!
He reaches, and
she grabs his hand ...
She's lifted to the sky ...

So on the back of paper birds
the girl and boy take flight.
The land of snow
speeds past below.
She has to ask him ...

'RIGHT ...

... WHAT JUST HAPPENED?

We're flying! On the backs of paper birds!'
And Hansel's speech unscrolls: 'You haven't heard?'

'Heard what?' asks Elsa, peeking at the ground,
where frosty Jack is pacing round and round.

Now Hansel turns. 'I can't get Gretel free.
She's trapped inside the castle grounds. You see,
Jack Frost has caught the mighty Shadowmaster!
If we don't stop him, then it spells disaster!'

'A ... Shadowmaster?' Elsa asks. 'What's that?
A person, or a thing? We need it back?'

'A person,' says the boy, and points: 'That tower.
We badly need the Shadowmaster's power.
Without it, we're all frozen in the past.
We can't move forward, can't make stories last.'

She frowns, and thinks it through. 'That isn't right!'
He takes her hand in his, so thin and light.

He says, 'There's something odd – in your world, too.
So Elsa, help us, please. The answer's ... *you*.'

Elsa's eyes ping open into the fairy-lit room:

into the *normal, three-dimensional* bedroom,

which smells of cosy old attics and *normality* …

She breathes deep twice, three times.

She's a bit sweaty, and the taste of the dream

is still in her mouth, and her fists are clenched.

It *had* been a dream, hadn't it? She blinks and stretches in the morning light, and hears the comforting sounds of Dad boiling the kettle in the kitchen.

But …

there,
scrunched in her fist …
something real …
A twist of paper! She uncrumples it, reads
the tiny letters, cut out so the light shines through:

PLEASE HELP

Chapter 6

Elsa's confused by the dream.
She remembers the feel of riding on those paper geese,
her hands touching their dry feathers,
and the silent rocking motion of their flight.
In her heart she knows that she must get back
inside the Shadowlands to help.
But ... how? She thinks of Jack Frost and shivers.
How can she get past *him*?
How can she find her way inside that shadowy tower?
And free this 'Shadowmaster' Hansel told her about ...
It seems impossible – as impossible as ... as a girl becoming paper!

And worse: she makes her bleary way downstairs
and opens the door to the shop.
All over the floor in front of the shadow theatre
are miniscule pieces of paper,
ripped and torn into tiny little snowflakes ...
The paper scraps of Elsa's paper geese!
'No!' It must have been Jack Frost ...!

She stands up, determined,
looking about the toyshop shelves, grasping for ideas.
Puppets, wooden horses, knitted animals ...
A dog made of wool peers out from behind a carved wooden bear ...
And then there are the books ...
Tips on painting puppets and making dolls' houses ...
They all seem useless!

Except ... One catches her eye.

There on the shelf is a book with shadows on its spine.

The phone in the flat upstairs starts ringing at that second –
and then the ringing abruptly stops. She can hear Dad's voice
floating down, and the way it starts out normal, and then gets
quieter   and quieter   and quieter.
Then there are his footsteps on the stairs
and the door of the shop gently opens.

'Elsa?'
    'Yes, Dad?'

Dad runs a hand through his hair, like he does when he's worried.
'That was the hospital. Everything's alright,
but I think it's best if you come with me this time.
I'm not sure how long I'll be out today.'

'Oh ...!'

Elsa pushes the shadow book back onto the shelf, but Dad says,
'No, bring a book. It might be a little while.'
So Elsa runs and gets her bag and packs: chocolate,
a carton of juice, the scissors, some paper, a sharp pencil,
and the shadow book.

The waiting room is the colour of flour, of milk,
of things that don't have a strong flavour of their own.
Elsa sits on a sofa that squeaks grumpily whenever she moves.
There are posters on the noticeboards,
splodgy pictures of nowhere on the walls,
and tired old magazines on the table. Nothing much for kids.
Elsa finds herself wishing for the toyshop and the flat.
Dad's in the next little room with Grandma;
Elsa can't hear anything through the door.
Instead, for now, she turns to the shadow book.

The pages are yellowing, the spine cracked – but
as she turns the pages, the silhouettes in it are fresh, magical.
There are delicate coaches pulled by horses,
exotic plants stretching through lattice-walls.
There are underwater scenes
with coral and seaweed swaying in the waves,
as fine as lace. There are starry-dark night skies
and bright-painted dawns; there are fancy dances
and sumptuous feasts and enticing forest villages …
The whole of fairytale is there,
in shadows against sunset-coloured backdrops,
and even as Elsa looks at the pictures her mind is drawn
towards them, thinking of the Shadowlands.

She remembers the feeling in her dream-that-wasn't-a-dream
of being

        shrunk
        as thin
        as a piece
        of paper.

There, in the Shadowlands, danger lurks
in the spiky form of Jack Frost.

But *here*, in the shadow book in her lap,
everything seems wondrous.
This is somewhere she would love to visit!
Yes, this is more like it!

So – how can she free the Shadowmaster?

She flicks through the pages, looking for inspiration,
for something fierce and powerful. *There!*
A warrior, to defeat Jack Frost!

Using a pencil, Elsa starts to copy the shape of the warrior,
trying to follow the edges of the young woman's helmet,
her armour. But her fingers are clumsy,
and she keeps getting the line wrong.
She wants to create things as beautiful as this,
but her hands are letting her down.

'RARH! It's no good!'

She yells in frustration, flings the pencil on the floor
and glances up just in time to see Dad,
who's opened the door and is looking at her funny.
She smiles, a bit embarrassed,
but his smile back has a lot of worry in it. He says,
'Elsa, darling, Grandma wants to say hello to you.'

Elsa suddenly feels shy.
'But ... What will I say to her?'

At this, Dad smiles a proper smile.
'Oh *really*, Elsa – as if you've ever had a problem
thinking of something to say! Come on in.
She's looking forward to seeing you.'
So Elsa follows him through
the porridge-coloured door, feeling   very   small.

There on the narrow white bed is Grandma –
her skin wrinkled as a well-used map,
her hair a cloud, her arms looking peaceful.
But it is her blazing brown eyes
that Elsa notices most.

'Hello, Grandma. It's me ... it's Elsa.'

At that, Grandma smiles a big, warm smile
like a thousand birthday-cake candles.

'As if I would not know my own, dear Elsa!
I'd know you anywhere,
no matter how many years go by.
It does me good to see you, girl.
Come here. Sit.'

Grandma's voice isn't loud, but it does not shake.
Elsa finds herself smiling back, and the last of her shyness melts
like snow in sunshine. She takes a seat on Grandma's bed,
and sees Grandma noticing the shadow drawing in her hand.

'What have you got there?'

'I'm trying to make something that will ...'
How can she explain?
'I'm trying to copy from the shadow book.
But it's difficult.'

Grandma gives a little chuckle.

'Ahhh, so you like shadow work?'

Elsa thinks. 'I love it, but it's sort of creepy, too.
And nothing comes out the way I want.'

>'So you just need to practise!
>Start small, and you will get better.
>I already heard about your triumph with the geese!'

For a moment Elsa's mind flashes back to the ride
on the back of the paper geese with Hansel.
Is *that* what Grandma means?

But Grandma says,

>'Your father told me how good you were
>making those paper birds, how quick.'

And Dad's smiling too, from his corner by the window.
And outside Elsa can see that snow is falling again:
real snow, over the mysterious town …

It makes her think of the snowy Shadowlands,
and the danger lurking there, and worry twists her mouth.
She looks up, and Grandma's looking back at her, eyes bright.

>'Here, let me see what you are working on.'

Elsa holds up the paper shyly.
'It isn't very good. I went wrong.'

'It *is* a good start! But the Warrior-Maiden isn't easy.
Why not begin with something a little quicker. Like …
a snowflake? The great thing about snowflakes
is that no two are the same, so a snowflake that *you* make
is *your* snowflake, real and true – and it can never be wrong!'

'A … snowflake?' It sounds complicated to Elsa.

Grandma nods firmly, then tells Elsa how to do it,
folding the paper into squares first,
then cutting out small shapes.
Grandma's eyes light up when she sees the old scissors
in Elsa's hands. And Elsa is surprised that after just a few snips
she can unfold the paper to reveal a lifelike, lacy snowflake,
so much more beautiful than she would have thought.

'It worked!'

Grandma does a chuckle which, half-way through,
turns into a yawn.

'See? Perfect. Now
I'm getting tired, but if you're quick
I can tell you how to make a lantern.
Fold that sheet in half – that's right …'

Elsa snips the paper here and there, as Grandma says,
and suddenly in her hand there's a lantern,
so lifelike she expects it to glow.

Chapter 7

Back at the flat, Elsa has had several ideas, all at once.
Her brain fizzes and pops with them.

It's already afternoon. It feels like there's too much to do
before the sunset washes over the rooftops
and it's dark again. *The Shadow Time*. Elsa shivers –
if it goes as planned, this will be a big, big test for her
and her new skills. But she thinks she can do this –
to protect herself, to free this Shadowmaster,
to unfreeze the stories ... So her scissors

snip   snip   snip   snip

And some of the snips don't go as Elsa meant,
but others do, and as time passes
more and more of the snips begin to make the shapes
that Elsa wanted. Simple shapes, at first, like Grandma said.
She is stacking up a little pile of things that she hopes
might help in that frozen land.

Mittens, a paper chain, a lantern ...
She cuts them from the paper,
and places them neatly on the carpet.

Then, when it's truly dusk, she curls up on her quilted bed,
knowing that she has to get to sleep now. She's nervous
and determined. She squeezes her eyes tight, but it won't work:
she needs to try something else ... so instead, she lies
looking up at the lamplit snowflakes falling one-by-one
on the sky-light, and counts them ...
One, two, three, four, five, six, seven, eight ... too many to count ...
and slowly, slowly ... she

                floats

                          away.

This time, it is not voices that wake her, but silence.
No voices call. There is no sound at all, in fact.
Elsa's eyes are wide in the lamplight.
She's still on her bed, but there are not the usual whisperings
from the toyshop downstairs signalling to her
that the Shadowlands adventures are about to start.
Puzzled, and a little spooked, she reaches down
for Grandma's slippers, and slips them on.

The eerie silence follows her through her bedroom,
and in the same way that there's no sound downstairs,
she realises she is not making any sound herself!
Not even her own footsteps ...
it sends a spider-shiver down her spine.
But there's nothing for it!
She has to follow the glow under the door of the toyshop,
to find the shadow theatre and its mysteries.

The Shadowlands glow with the light of the moon
on the snow – but now nothing is right.
The landmarks she saw in the scenery have gone,
and they've all been replaced with blank white.

The snow's piled up high – so much higher than it was –
and the earth is chilled down to the core.
'Jack Frost made it colder!' she says, and the words
cut themselves from the sky, like before.

She's stamping and clapping for warmth, while her breath
billows from her, and mists up her way.
But then she remembers the first of the shapes
that she made in her bedroom today.

'Mittens!' she says, and she finds on her hands
little mittens, and feels a bit better.
Her paper hands warmer, she's ready to start …
(She'd been asked to … '*PLEASE HELP*' … in that letter.)

She must find the tower, that ice-bitten castle
where Jack Frost has locked up his guests.
Elsa must free them: this strange Shadowmaster
and Gretel … She *must* do her best …

She calls the name of the friend she knows
in this frozen land of ice and snow.

'HANSEL!
HANSEL!'

Elsa wanders east and west –
but doesn't know which way is best.

'HANSEL!
HANSEL!'

The shadows creep without a sound.
Oh, *where* is Hansel to be found?

'HANSEL!
HANSEL!'

'*It's you!*' begins a frosty voice.
Jack's suddenly right there:
*'It must be clear
the boy's not here!
He could be – anywhere!'*

The frosty villain chucks away
an empty ice-cream cone.
Elsa shies
from those ice-eyes,
chilly to the bone.

'You've come without your friend!' says Jack.
'In this place, that's not clever!
So you must stay;
not just today:
you'll live here – oh, FOREVER.'

And Jack Frost traps the girl in ice!
She shouts out – 'HELP!' – but in a trice
they're skating fast! No geese! No Hansel!
No time at all before they've reached

                      the icy,

                            chilling,

                                  frosted,

                                        lonely

                                            castle!

The castle	stretches up into the snow-heavy clouds above.
The castle	is topped with battlements, all spiked and glittery.
The castle	is the loneliest place Elsa has ever seen.

Elsa	cannot get away from chilly Jack Frost.
Elsa	wishes she had made some sort of paper snow-plough!
Elsa	wants to wake up in her cosy bed, and realise this was all a dream.

Statues	made of ice are frozen around the castle grounds.
Statues	that resemble fairytale characters: Red Riding Hood, the Wolf ...
A statue	that looks exactly like ... *HANSEL?!*
Elsa	is still in Jack's icicle as he hurries her through the garden, into the castle.
Elsa	tries to remember the route he's taking her, but it's turn after turn.
Elsa	is led up twisting ice-glittering steps, towards the tallest tower.
Jack Frost	looks like he's really enjoying himself.
Jack Frost	is glowing bluer, colder by the minute.
Jack Frost	is singing a creepy little song. It goes like this:

> *'Oh! When the Shadowmaster's frozen*
> *and that power's mine ...*
> *That's it! Watch out!*
> *I'll TAKE TIME OUT! ...*
> *I'll FREEZE the whole of TIME!'*

And as Jack Frost is saying this,
he conjures an ice lolly –
scoffs it, flicks
the lolly-stick,
and rubs his icy belly.

'*LOOK!*' he says, and skates her to
a window, close at hand.
Far below
she sees, she knows:
the icy statues stand.

And Elsa understands the truth!
He's *frozen* Hansel, then!
And all of them
are stuck! Oh, when
will *she* get home again?

'*Perfect! Perfect!*' says Jack Frost.
'*Their tales' power grows my own!*'
And Elsa shivers,
shakes and quivers,
chilled down to the bone.

'*Nearly, nearly,*' says cold Jack,
'*and then I'LL be Time's master!
It leaves just one
thing to be done:
I'll freeze – the Shadowmaster!*

The problem is,*' Jack mutters on,
'*I do admit, I fear her ...*'
'... Who? Let me free!'
says Elsa – 'please!'
But Jack seems not to hear her.

He leads her to a heavy door
reached by a spiral stair.
He shoves her in!
It's dark and grim:
no bed, no food, no chair.

'Just wait right here, you meddling child,'
Jack says. 'No more resistance!
You understand
my plans are grand ...
I don't want your "assistance"!'

'YOU CANNOT DO THIS!' Elsa shouts.
'Just did!' says frosty Jack.
'Boohoo! How sad!
Too late! Too bad!
Don't worry – I'LL BE BACK!'

There's just a window made of ice;
it's smooth, without a crack.
Jack locks the door:
once, twice, once more ...
and
now
the
girl
is
trapped.

Chapter 8

But Elsa's spirits don't *all* drop.
She's never been a girl who *stops*.

She needs to melt the ice around her,
somehow make some warmth surround her …

Her lantern! Yes! She says the word
and there it is, as if it *heard* …

The ice around her melts! Relieved,
she grabs the lantern firmly, heaves

it to the icy window-pane …
The window melts to air again!

It's opened up! She peers out … frowns
and groans to see the long way down!

She leans out in the morning air,
and hopes a friend might see her there …

'HELP!' calls Elsa. 'SOMEONE, ANSWER!
HALLO! HANSEL?
      HALLO! GRETEL?
            HALLO!' (She knows there's *someone* here …) –
                'HALLO, THE SHADOWMASTER?'

She listens in the morning frost,
feeling lonely, feeling lost ...
feeling silly ... feeling sillier ...
There's a voice!　　　　　　it's *quite* –　　　　　　familiar ...

　　　　　　　　'Elsa?'

'Yes, it's me! It's me!'
Elsa cranes, and tries to see.
'Shadowmaster? *Where are you?*'

　　　　　　'Elsa, no! Jack got you too?'

The words are floating down, quite near;
they're thin and small, but crystal-clear ...
A room nearby ... but where – *but where?*
The girl looks round her everywhere ...

　　　　　'Girl, you're not *safe* on your own!
　　　　　You mustn't risk it! Please go home!'

But Elsa won't accept a limit.
She paper-shouts: 'JUST WAIT A MINUTE!'

The Shadowmaster's power's what
Jack wants to get, but ...　　HE MUST NOT.

And Elsa knows what she must do:
she'll free herself – the Master too!

The trouble is this slippery Jack.
He's *bad!* ... Her puzzled mind slips back
and forth, and asks: *How can she send his
power away, and somehow END this?*

She's at the window. Where to go?
The problem's all this *snow on snow* ...
The mean wind drives the snowflakes in ...

    SO – THAT'S IT! Warm it!   *Make it SPRING!*

She sees a tree beneath her – there –
its empty branches in the air ...

She'll make it bloom! She rips a flake
of paper snow, and from it makes
more little shreds, and more, and more ...
creating blossom on the floor!

She throws great handfuls of the flowers
down from her window in the tower ...

    and

            watches

                      wonderful

                                  spring

waking, stretching,   u n f u r l i n g.

And with it, Elsa's mind de-frosts again!
There's something else she made: the PAPER CHAIN!

And just like that, it's hanging on the wall!
She clambers down it, careful not to fall ...

She's made it to the garden safely! Yes!
But now there comes a bigger, harder test ...

Spring is waking as she goes, and so
her footsteps melt behind her through the snow.

And with her blows a springtime breeze
which grows bright blossom on the trees.
And far above, the deep-grey sky
is turning blue, and young birds fly
between the gently gliding clouds ...
The air is filled with springtime sounds ...

She hurries to the statue-place,
and finds the one with Hansel's face.
He thaws at Elsa's touch; asks 'Who ...?'
'It's Elsa! Me! I'm rescuing you!'

And Hansel blinks again, then laughs,
and sweeps her up with him, to dance.

And Elsa whoops for joy ... then calms,
and twists away from Hansel's arms.

'We have to go ... I need to free
the Shadowmaster ... come with me!'

'First Gretel! Quick – she's somewhere near ...'
And taking Elsa's hand, he steers
her through the frozen-statue-park,
past people who've become landmarks.

And as they go, brave Elsa spreads
her magic petals on their heads,
and statues stir, and stretch, and sigh,
and smile up at the sunlit sky.

But where is Gretel? Not among
the trees or shrubs – not on the lawn ...

Not on the frozen garden steps,
nor boathouse, greenhouse, woodstore, shed ...

Elsa blinks, and chokes back tears.
At *this* rate, they might search for *years*!

They unfreeze frozen faces, fast,
both near and far – until, at last ...

'*There* Gretel is!' says Hansel then.
'Please wake my sister up again!'

Jack's kept frozen Gretel hidden
at the centre of a *fountain*!

A sprinkle of the paper blooms
and Gretel wakes, and beams, and zooms
to Hansel, hugs him very tight – till:
'*Off!*' he laughs. 'You're soggy, Gretel!'

But now she's hugging Elsa too.
'*You're* the one – we needed *you*!
Thank you, thank you! When I fell
asleep, I *hoped* you'd break the spell!'

'Well done!' says Hansel. 'Now ... we've got
to foil Jack Frost's outrageous plot ...
The Master's in the castle tower ...
but how to free her, and her power?'

> So Elsa tries to think like Jack.
> 'There's *some* way to convince him ...
> I'll *make* him. *He*
> will set her free.
> I'll use his tricks against him!'

Chapter 9

It doesn't take young Elsa long
to run back. None can stop her
as she climbs again
the paper chain,
and grabs a scrap of paper.

She rolls it in a makeshift cone
and stuffs it to the seams
with paper balls.
She hopes Jack falls
for this ... a fake ice cream!

And then – so very carefully! –
she climbs out of her prison,
swings the chain
around again
and makes a quick decision ...

She creeps towards a window, which
is big, and grand, and glittery.
Jack, she'd guess,
would not want less!
She feels a little jittery ...

Inside, Jack's sitting on a throne
he's made of snow and frost.
(But Elsa thinks,
despite these things,
he looks a little ... lost?)

She puts that thought aside, and lifts
the ice cream in the air.
Its shadow streams
in inky beams
above Jack's sparkling chair.

'What's THIS?' asks Jack, and stands up quick
to scrutinise it better.
'An icy treat?
But not to eat ...'
His stare's so cold it glitters.

Elsa, on the windowsill,
can barely dare to breathe.
If he works out
what she's about,
he'll rage, he'll shout, he'll seethe!

'Fine craftsmanship,' he says at last.
'I shouldn't put it past her.
There's ONE who could
make work this good.
It's her ... MUST be ... could only ever be ... of course ... quite definitely ...
the SHADOWMASTER!

I'll pay a visit to my guest.
She must be working spells.
I don't know what
she's thinking, but
this might not end so well!'

Elsa scarcely dares to blink,
but inside, she's *so* hopeful!
Her plan is working!
Jack is walking
out, and through the castle!

Elsa follows, quiet as snow,
not *sure* what she expects there ...
But knowing that
he's dangerous, Jack ...
She *hopes* he won't detect her!

She tiptoes through the corridors
and stares around in wonder ...
When Jack unlocks
a cell door: SHOCK!

The Shadowmaster's ...
GRANDMA!

And when she sees her, Elsa knows
how courage, like an oak tree, grows
from something weak – but grows up STRONG.
Did Elsa sense this, all along?

She *thought* she knew that voice, before!
She smiles, and sneaks behind the door.
And as she goes, she *almost* thinks
that Grandma winks the teeniest,   tiniest   of   winks.

'You'd better stop these games right now!'
Jack Frost declares, to Grandma;
'I will not fall
for TRICKS – that's all
your magical displays are!'

But Grandma yawns, and merely blinks,
not fussed at all by what he thinks.
    'Oh, shadows playing tricks again?'
she says, with something like disdain.

'Stop it!' says Jack Frost, and twirls
the key that locks her prison.
'Hour by hour
your shadow power
is MESSING with my VISION!'

'Oh,' says Grandma. 'Is that so?
You can't work spells or freeze me? No?
Jack, bad news: your magic's faulty.
That's the price of being ... oh,
I really can't be bothered to think up a rhyme,' she ends,

and Elsa feels a little thrill
that Grandma's breaking all the rules!

'So,' continues Grandma, 'Jack,
there's something you could learn from that ...'

Elsa, from her hideout, spies
her grandma half-wink one bright eye.

'Nothing interests me ...' sniffs Jack,
'... except a world that's blizzardy –
a world of cold,
a world that's chilled,
a world of – PURPLE CHICKENS!'

Jack looks a little panicky
and tries again, more frantically:

'I mean ... a world of ... of ... FANCY PIGEONS!
No, wait ... JELLY BRIDGES!
Friendly fridges ...! Cosy ... mittens? Playful kittens?
NO! It's your stupid POWER getting to me! I MEAN!
A world of FROSTY MISERY!'

Elsa's trying not to laugh,
and not to faint – it's half and half.

'Yes,' says Grandma, wearily.
'The *chickens* thing was news to me,
but all that stuff – you've mentioned it:
the *blizzards*, and the *misery* bit ...

> But – by the way – I'll put you right
> on your most glaring oversight.
> You see, Jack Frost, it isn't *me*
> who's tricking you so splendidly ...'

And Elsa feels a glow, and knows.
It's now or never ... so: HERE GOES!

'It's *me*!' she says, and Jack Frost spins
upon the spot, and looks so grim
that Elsa feels her heart quake. But
she bravely screws her courage up ...

'You oaf! You didn't realise
that lovely SPRING has sprung outside!'

> *'Spring?!'* gasps Jack, and with a leap
> he's peering from the window.
> *'No no! It can't!*
> *It shan't! Yuk, yuk!*
> *The warmth would not only melt my STATUES; it would also be*
> *really terrible for my general plan to FREEZE everything!'*

Now, behind his glittering back,
> wise Grandma sneaks away from Jack!
>> Grandma's calm and cool and tough ...
>>> But still she's not quite *fast* enough.

And next there comes an icy rage ...
and Elsa feels a huge cold cage
claw round and through them. Elsa knows then:
all is lost, 'cause Time is frozen.

But just that second, Elsa thinks
some cosy thoughts: of warming drinks,
and sunny days, and hugs – so nice!
And stops *herself* becoming ice.

So Elsa gathers all her might,
grabs Grandma's hand, and pulls her right
out – through the open, frosted door,
along the frozen corridor ...

straight down the staircase, from the top –
Jack's cottoned on, and screams out '*Stop!*'
She hears him yell ... he's catching up ...
He skates so fast – they're out of luck!

She stumbles, skids, and almost trips ...
Jack throws a ball of snow, which hits
the wall just by her head. Then one
flies by her leg. They run – run – run!

By now they've reached the ground floor, where
the frost-lights froze mid-flicker. They're
not sure if it is night or day,
with shadows round them caught mid-sway.

But Grandma, Elsa sees, is weak,
and doesn't shout, and doesn't speak.
And Elsa knows time's running out
to save themselves, while Jack's about ...

But then she feels a small hope dart
inside her mind, or in her heart:
a voice she's sure she's always known,
that's hers, just hers – her very own.

> *Dream about the happiest place,*
> *it says. Dream Dad. Dream Aisha's face.*
> *Dream paper geese. Dream shadow fun.*
> *Dream Grandma's smile, bright as the sun.*
> *Dream old, dream home. Dream new, dream far.*
> *Dream ELSA – just the way you are.*

And Elsa opens up her eyes
(she hadn't known she'd closed them), spies
the exit, with the sunny day
beyond – and dives ... the *other* way!

Jack, behind them, swerves and skids,
trips over   his clumsy skates,   and   slips

and Elsa, panting, sees her chance.
'LAMP!' she shouts, and all at once
she holds the lantern, source of light
and heat, and everything that's *right*.

She runs with Grandma – way past Jack ...
Then Elsa has a thought, turns back
and holds the lantern right up high,
against the bright-blue springtime sky.

Jack Frost's recovered, on his feet,
and skates towards her, snarling, *'Cheat!'*

The lantern in her hands glows bright
as Jack Frost hurtles to the light …

His mouth's a twist of spiky anger.
In his eyes are sparks of danger.

> But Jack's no match for Elsa's lamp.
> His frozen magic's getting – damp!

> > Braver than she's ever felt,
> > she sees his rage begin to MELT!

> > > 'Wow!' says Grandma. 'Clever Elsa!
> > > Now we *all* know *you're* the Master!'

Elsa stands up tall, and grins.
She feels she can do ANYTHING.

'Gedoff!   Begone!   Go 'way!   Get lost!'
attempts the furious Jack Frost …

but Spring light's melting everything …
His magic just won't work for him!

And in that warm light, steaming, puffing,
Jack shrinks down to almost nothing …

Snowman-size at first, then snowball,
lump to *handful* to *light snowfall* ...

Till he is so snowflake-small
he hardly seems that bad at all ...

      But ...

The snowflake-that-was-Jack squeaks meanly,
shakes his mini fist so keenly,
trying different spells ... and so
quick Elsa picks him up – and blows ...

and
      puffs
            away
                  the
                        tiny
                              thing
towards the Time-thawed sky of Spring.

'Shoo!' she tells him. 'Off you go!
We'll call you back when we need   more   *snow*!'

Time flows again, and Jack's defeated!
Icy reigns won't be repeated!
Now's a time of huge elation!
Elsa leads the celebrations!

'We're FREE!' She dances up and down
with Gretel. Hansel jumps around.
Red Riding Hood is laughing, whirling!
The Big Bad Wolf is (sort of) twirling!

But Elsa knows she can't stay long –
she thinks of lights, like fairies, strung
above her bed. They're on her mind.
They seem to say: *it's time, it's time.*

She hugs the others, one by one;
spies Grandma, sitting in the sun,
and feels pride, mixed with other things,
for that wise lady, here, in Spring.

'Come on, Grandma.

Time to go home.'

She holds out her hand to Grandma,
who (Elsa notices) looks frail,
and tired,
as if she were made
of not much more
than paper.

'Elsa   darling –
I'm sorry.'

Grandma has not taken Elsa's hand.

Elsa stands, still waiting.

'What are you sorry for?' she asks. 'Come on!'

Grandma smiles a complicated smile –
a smile with as much sadness in it
as happiness.

'I can't   come with you.   How I wish I could.
I must stay   here.'

'WHAT?' says Elsa.
Grandma nods, firmly.

Elsa grabs her hand,
and it feels light as a dream.

'This is where   I belong now.'

'But I need you, Grandma!
I couldn't have done this without you!'

'All of this   was *you*.
Don't worry,   sweetheart.
I'll be   right   here   always.'

Elsa tries to pull Grandma towards her ...
She feels the loosening grip of Grandma's papery hand ...

And then she's holding onto nothing at all,
and she's upstairs, under the quilt, in her warm bed,
lit by fairylights ...
And under the skylight, which is covered
in morning-coloured snow.

And Elsa knows something true. She knows that the world
is real, and huge, and wonderful, and sometimes sad.
And just as she's thinking this, the phone rings, and a little later
there's a knock at her bedroom door.   It's Dad.
'Love ...' he starts, and Elsa knows from the way he says it
what he means.

'She's gone, isn't she? Grandma?' Dad nods slowly, once,
and Elsa feels a great flood of love and sadness
and – somewhere at the back of it all –
something shining, like a little lantern.
Something she can't name, but which glows there, quiet.

She jumps out of bed and hugs Dad tight, tight, tight,
and she can tell it's helping him as much as it's helping her.
He sniffs, and says, 'She wanted you to keep these for your own.'
Dad hands Elsa something metallic and intricate ...

'The *Shadowmaster*'s scissors!' says Elsa, remembering,
as her hand closes round the glinting metal,

and the tools fit her

perfectly.

Now answer the questions ...

1. What did Elsa's dad hang up in her room?

2. Why did Elsa think messages in her mind to her best friend Aisha (for example on page 20)?

3. 'The earth is frost, and wintry trees criss-cross the paths like filigree' (page 28). What does 'filigree' mean?

4. Why do you think the author chose to write some of the story in non-rhyming free verse, and some of it in rhyming verse?

5. On page 51, Jack said 'Just wait right here, you meddling child' – what does 'meddling' mean?

6. What did you think would happen when Elsa tried to trick Jack Frost with the paper ice cream?

7. How do you think Elsa changed from the start of the story to the end?

8. Have you read a story in verse, like this one, before? What sort of rhyming structure(s) did it use?